| DATE | | | |
|---|---|---|---|
|  |  |  |  |
|  |  |  |  |
|  |  |  |  |
|  |  |  |  |
|  |  |  |  |
|  |  |  |  |
|  |  |  |  |
|  |  |  |  |
|  |  |  |  |
|  |  |  |  |
|  |  |  |  |
|  |  |  |  |

# Green Again

# Green Again

Betsy Barber Bancroft

Illustrated by Ruth Powers Bridges

PELICAN PUBLISHING COMPANY
GRETNA, 1972

Manufactured in the United States by the
TJM Corporation, Baton Rouge, Louisiana.
Typography by Forstall Typographers
Published by Pelican Publishing Company, Inc.
630 Burmaster Street, Gretna, Louisiana 70053

*For Joe*

## Preface

Poetry is, to me, a sort of springtime in man's experience. In poetry, as in unhindered nature, whatever has been green will be so again or will beget another greenness. Those experiences which man recorded in poetry ages ago will present new blossoms in new lights and shadows for the eyes of today.

Because each year has a spring and yet every spring is a new and different one; because poetry is brought forth again and again as new men find the old experiences and initiate new ones; and because both of these springtimes are gifts of God and as such can not be diminished, even by the harshest winters, this, my second book, must be GREEN AGAIN.

— Betsy Barber Bancroft

## Acknowledgments

The education, inspiration and encouragement received from the real poet in the family, my father, William C. Barber, have been invaluable to the progress of this collection.

"The bark flower" and "On the loss" are reprinted from POEM, March 2, 1968 by permission of the publisher.

"Action" is from THE SAMPLER of the Alabama State Poetry Society and is reprinted by their permission.

*And now, my friends, all that is true, all that is noble, all that is just and pure, all that is lovable and gracious, whatever is excellent and admirable—fill all your thoughts with these things.*

*Philippians 4:8*
*New English Bible*

*whatever has been green*

*The bark flower*

I found a place
where once a tree had stood.
Concentric shards
of tree and bark, rain-rusted, brown,
had made
a perfect-layered rose
without a stem.

The woods had laid
a wreath to testify
that years
of changing liveliness
and days of death
were time unwasted if
that woods-floor blossom were
their only worth.

And who can say
that what remained
was not a flower.

### Never a secret place

There was a secret hill
I sought in sleep
where no one walked
and memory was live,
a haven where
my crowded heart withdrew.
A road bent downward
from a shady knoll,
an echo haunted constantly
its end,
and somewhere, far beyond
and out of sight,
slow, quiet people moved
with muted steps.
Love's memory was there,
not loneliness.

Bright trees, dark-dappled trees
with cooling leaves,
so many trees, remembering,
and stones . . .
stones, dust and waking sounds
of many birds,
a bank where roses tumbled
trailing down,
and all the buds were mine,
smooth for my hands,
pale for my eyes,
mine for my hidden heart.

*Always when I awoke*
*out of the dream*
*I knew the house*
*upon the hill was gone,*
*I knew the roads*
*had laid the tall trees down*
*and all the summer's gentle birds*
*had flown,*
*and then, last night,*
*while I was in the dream,*
*a crowd of people*
*thronged my quiet land*
*and there will never be*
*again for me*
*a secret place*
*where others may not go.*

### The costume

The woman
in the crinkled photograph
had borne the decades
with a regal mien
and wore with grace
the costume of her day.

Her eyes told me
that we were deepest kin,
then with a shock
I recognized
the crowning item
of her haute couture.

She wore my nose,
my straight and
no-more-nonsense
narrow nose.

It was a perfect nose
for wearing then,
(when boots and collars
closed up tight and high)
but lacks the tilt
for mores of today.

Still I am pleased
to have the nose of one
who wore her velvets
and her disciplines
with such aplomb.

## A Funeral

Old Nonnie Moon had fallen on the floor.
The doctor came and said that she had passed.
Someone took Nonnie's body in a hearse.
They painted Nonnie's face
and combed her hair.
Then all the family went by to see.
Her children held up well
because they thought
that Nonnie looked just like she was asleep.

Her preacher lives in Crane and couldn't come.
Someone real nice said he would read graveside.

The sun was hot.
It was a lovely day.

Four young, black men were digging Nonnie's grave.
When they were through
they crossed the road to rest
and eat their lunch beside a poplar tree.
There in the shade they sat,
and laughed
and talked.

The grave was
just a hole
out in the sun.

*At almost one,*
*inside the shiny box,*
*the body waited*
*for the time to come*
*for everyone to gather*
*and begin.*

*The diggers stood*
*and waited by their tree.*
*They did not watch.*
*They had to fill the hole.*

*Then Nonnie's children came.*
*Some of them cried*
*while friends and neighbors watched*
*and sympathized.*
*The preacher gave his Bible words*
*and prayers*
*and all the talk*
*about dear Nonnie's life.*
*Then some of Nonnie's grandchildren,*
*grown up,*
*were kissing friends,*
*and shaking hands around.*

*They thanked the minister*
*and everyone*
*and got into their cars*
*and drove away,*
*some of the older women crying still.*

They left the box
with Nonnie's body there
and someone let it down
into the ground.

A neighbor, Myrtle Hard,
went to her car.
She fluffed the white bed pillow on the seat
and turned to speak
to Nonnie's step-grand-niece.
"I have to have this pillow when I drive.
The seat's so hard and I'm so thin," she clucked.
"There's no meat on my hips."
She said it loud.
The step-grand-niece looked odd
and didn't speak,
so Myrtle, thinking that she hadn't heard,
said it again and smiled and drove away.

The laborers came back
and brought the dirt,
shoveled it down
on Nonnie's shiny box
until the hole was full
and then they left.

*On the loss*

*The early sounds*
*of colored voices fade away.*
*They have become a noise*
*to be despised by those*
*whose mouths have given*
*life and form to them.*

*Those voices, lively-sad,*
*remind of other time,*
*of other time*
*and sorry circumstance.*
*They will dissolve*
*to be replaced*
*by independencies*
*and random cries*
*of rising hate,*
*and I will miss*
*those gentle Negro noises*
*in the air.*
*They poured out*
*in a liquid tumble*
*to our ears,*
*like chocolate,*
*warm and dark,*
*rich as pure cream.*

No man who never heard
their summer laughs
or working talk
will know to mourn
that ebon smoothness
flowed away,
or all the careless,
run-together words —
soft, dusky pillows
thrown in disregard,
by all their great-eyed,
dark, brown
colored children.

*The difficulty*

*It is not hard*
*to understand*
*that people go away*
*or that they die.*
*What puzzles me*
*is that we cease to speak*
*their given names*
*and wear their faces*
*without memory.*

## Miss Charlotte Black

Charlotte,
a book of years left open at the place
where life engraved rich words on every line,
a story moving with such constant grace
no hateful letter mars the rare design
or stains the page with any sorrow's trace.

Charlotte,
a door to other days the present tries
and, finding welcome, enters in and dreams.
Past decades, dancing bright in Charlotte's eyes,
fill every open room with life that seems
not aged, and yet, not young but lively-wise.

Charlotte,
a fragile cup of liquid rich and sweet
enough to sip, to savor well and trust
there are not bitter dregs the lips must meet.
She keeps the memory of life's noon thrust
the way grapes garner all their strength from heat.

Charlotte,
a single flower on a slender stem.
With her are endless gardens, deathless leis
of green, remembered blooms, the scent of them
so sharply fresh it permeates her ways.
Though petals softly close they do not dim.

*Of Eve, past and present*

*—and what of Eve,*
*in the beginning,*
*what was her sin,*
*the first of so many?*
*The curiosity to listen*
*to the tempter,*
*or that she, hearing,*
*doubted God's intentions*
*toward her*
*and the one man?*

*No.*
*The poor, silly girl*
*refused*
*to exercise dominion,*
*that power of responsibility,*
*that responsibility of power*
*which God*
*had wanted Adam*
*and the woman*
*to enjoy.*

—and Eve today?
Still throwing away dominion,
telling her children
not to break the rules,
or else the doctor,
the teacher, the policeman,
that man, someone,
(anyone but her)
will get them,
(whatever that may mean),
and presently wheedling
her present Adam,
teasing him
to give up his dominion,
beginning with
his power over her,
wishing all the while
that he would say,
that he had said,
"Has not God said . . .?"

*Sequoiah encounter*

A giant tree was bred
in a forest of giants,
of an earth and an air
before man's memory.
Its dark head
like a grizzled tip
of arrow
was prodding sky
for room to lean on ether,
or so it seemed;
and as I watched,
a cobweb,
tenuous filament,
(from that day's spider)
blew, one end free,
and turned to fiery silver,
struck brilliant
in the late, limb-threading sun.
And I was there,
alive to that whole moment,
with a tree and many trees
that were the eons
and a web that was a moment—
and was, in coming, gone.

## The commitment

### I

I have been widowed by the time just passed
           and I am set aside.
All times possess the selves they apprehend.
I gave myself, as a virgin gives,
           to my first time,
            saving nothing, fully and finally.
I am not dead although that time is dead
                but I am given.

And I am glad I gave myself to such a time,
           when most men recognized
              that God is living in all times.
                We knew Him then,
                  and knew that we were His.

By grace (or by persistence,
          depending upon whose eyes
            are the sanctioned mirror)
        I keep within me the seeds
          of the quiet Sundays
         when people visited their friends and kinsmen
           without appointments,
      thinking themselves and others
            more valuable than time.

### II

All our blankets were moth-balled and scratchy
      and we were thankful to have them.
     They were so much warmer than cotton
        and we hadn't thought of synthetics.

We sent old coats and outgrown mittens,
        by boat, to flood refugees in Europe
          who probably were frozen
             before the clothing arrived.

At least we tried and surely someone there
        would be alive and cold enough to use them
          even a year or two late.

### III

We all picked violets, as soon as they were blooming,
        and took them to Lillie Stone's mother.
Lil, as blond as an angel, had been five and a half that winter.
        She died of double pneumonia
          just as spring was beginning.
They said it was from wading
        in the branch with us that April
          and they never let us forget it.
      (That's what always happens to children
        who wade
          before the adults are warm enough.)
Mrs. Stone showed us Lillie's picture and cried
            so we cried too.
She put the violets in Lil's little china tea pot
        to wilt on the dresser doily
          by Lil's last smiling picture.
I don't know whether or not it helped
        but we did it every year
          for as long as we were together.

## IV

In summertime we sweated.
    Nobody seemed to resent it.
        Sometimes we went with buckets
            to the green and dusty country,
          in spite of the snakes and the brambles,
            to pick the wild blackberries.

The ice-boxes were heroic,
      electric but inefficient,
         so some of us got food poisoning
            from eating potato salad.
Some of us died of things like typhoid fever
         and the rest of us knew somehow
            that it couldn't be helped.

We sprayed down our throats
        and up our noses
           with medicine (greenish-yellow)
        to keep from catching polio.

We washed our dishes
      without rubber gloves,
     did our yard work
         and washing and ironing
    and drank iced tea
    with sugar
      and mint
        and lemon.

Our hands were not smooth
        but we cried more at funerals.
        We didn't contain ourselves.
          It didn't seem necessary.

Once when I saw a fist fight
        in front of a corner drugstore
         my heart and stomach
               both went sick
   because two grown men were hurting one another
                  on purpose.

## V

Sometimes we'd hear of someone's
        running away with someone else's wife
            or husband.
They always had the grace to be embarrassed
        and they didn't advertise it.
Many of us believed that one man and one woman
        could belong to each other forever
          (or at least until one of them died)
      and that they could be happy together.
We saw them do it.

## VI

I still belong to that dead time
　　　　and that live God
　　　　　　and I will not forget it.

I will not smile with today's found people
　　　　who talk of second hand orgies and vices
　　　　　　culled and remembered and cherished
　　　　　　　　from printed and pictured obscenities
　　　　　　while their odorless, pillow-soft bodies
　　　　sit neatly arranged in the clothing
　　　　　　　made and maintained by machines.

They are living by proxy,
　　　　　explaining that life is like that now
　　　　　　　and that I should accept it.

I don't believe it.

Some life may be like that
　　　　　but not the life I'm given to.
It's not so simple a matter as not conforming.
It's just that you can give away virginity
　　　　　　　of any kind
　　　　　　　　but once.

*Unspeakable*

They never say good-bye.
Whatever else is said
they mean farewell.

They hold us
with their quiet, waiting hands
and tell us we are young,
and beautiful,
and give them light.

They never say good-bye.
With many other words they say
"I'm going now.
Keep me to earth.
I know no other place."

The words they use
mean nothing less.
They never say good-bye.

*another greenness*

Green again

Some poets find spring songs irrelevant.
                I have to laugh
                            (or cry) at such a thought.
Knowing that what we say,
                or fail to say,
                            can not deter the resurrecting earth
                            what can men do but sing?

Spring comes
                and comes
                and comes,
                            though weary men
                                will drop away this year.
A poet may be dying in this hour.
                            Many are living-dying,
                                many dead;
                but wild vines, green again
                on all the hills,
                            syrup the moving air.

Despite what man has thought
                            and said
                            and done
                the spring has come again
                this very year.

*Impact*

A bird in flight had flung himself
against the wide glass of my sunlit room
and there upon the pane
a dusty, dry bird-print remained
in spite of rains and winds
and other rains.
His wings and breast, his head,
his fragile beak and slender claws,
all that he was
translated into powder-print
where light shone straight
upon the glass.

What man can hope to leave, when he is gone,
more than the faintest trace
where he has hurled himself full force at life?

*Images*

*There are no mountains*
*rising in men's minds*
*that do not, somewhere,*
*wait beside earth's plains.*

*There are no springing waters*
*in our dreams*
*that do not course*
*some way which has been drawn*
*through rocks and milleforming trees.*

*There are no flowers,*
*lifting bright and sweet*
*within our hearts,*
*which were not long ago*
*deep-rooted on some distant secret isle.*

### Retort

I hear the strident harpy voices call
"Come, come away
and leave your chosen place!"

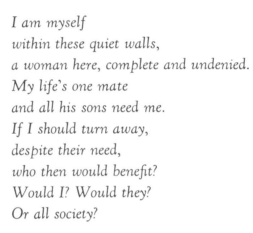

I am myself
within these quiet walls,
a woman here, complete and undenied.
My life's one mate
and all his sons need me.
If I should turn away,
despite their need,
who then would benefit?
Would I? Would they?
Or all society?

The woman-treasure
of a godly man,
I build with him,
though slowly, other men
whose lives, someday, will
curse or bless the land
by what our hands and hearts
can work in them.

If one good man
can discipline his way
to love me
and protect me from the world
and give me strength
and sustenance and joy,
can come to lie with me
alone at night,
and several sons
ask me to teach them life,
all else shall wait,
all poorer things pass by.

How could I choose to emulate a man?
God made me something else He said is good.

*Late prayer*

Oh, God,
      I hope there are some men
          who never read the news.

Somewhere
        there must be
          one small boy
             who doesn't open mail,
         a few old ladies
           (blind and deaf)
               who do remember pictures of themselves,
              especially their eyes,
                 when they were twenty-one,
          and who don't ever watch
            the talk shows in the evening.

Isn't there
      a single unrelenting drunk
      who hasn't understood
         what the street boys are requesting?

Protect them, God,
        from the bitter-metal eyes of youth.
Keep them, Father,
      from the diamond faces
         of our twelve year old women.

*Professionalism*

*Harry Fuller boasted.*
　　*He swelled and smiled and waited*
　　　*for earned congratulations.*
　*He had made a wooded,*
　　*troublesomely rocky,*
　　　*flower infested hillside*
　　　　*as flat and smooth and useful*
　　　　　*as any ping-pong table.*

*Marcia Samek, poet,*
　　*fed words to a computer,*
　　　*(vocabulary, grammar*
　　　　*and patterns for the stanzas)*
　　*then wrote a criticism*
　　　*of the poetry it gave her.*

*Lisa killed a woman*
　　*with forty-seven stab wounds.*
　　*She sat all through her trial*
　　*with eyes hard-dry, explaining*
　　*that she had been*
　　　*no more than a machine*
　　*before she took up murder*
　　　*to drive away her boredom.*
　　　　*. . . and what is blood?*

*Origin*

*I know*
*my spirit*
*crossed*
*the reach*
*of time,*
*past*
*the mute*
*eyelessness*
*of night,*
*down avenues*
*of breathless*
*stellar day.*

*I have not,*
*in entirety,*
*sprung*
*from the slime*
*of nether sea.*
*God and His universe*
*sing in my heart*
*and thunder*
*in my brain.*

## The smile

In hurrying today
I saw a car flash by,
one of the hundreds
on a large highway.
The man who drove it
did not see me pass.

His was the only smiling face
I saw among the shining lanes
where frowners hurried by.
His mouth was open
in an almost-laugh
and I could tell he thought
of tenderness and waiting love,
and it sustained him
in a hectic day.

I thank you, God
that I may go with him,
by love into his hardest day,
and for the many times
that he has said
that often, as he works,
he thinks of me
and smiles.

*A desert*
*is a harsh*
*and bitter thing.*

*Shall I be made ashamed*
*that I am,*
*to one man,*
*oasis*
*in the heat*
*of everyday?*

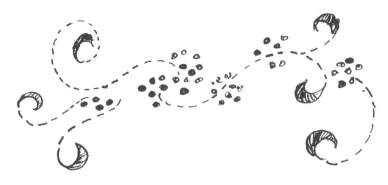

Action

Terrible groups of one
and sometimes more
are running backward fast
away from whatever fire.
They find me every time
with my bucket of unmixed answers
coming to fight the flame.

When they have looked
into the bucket and smiled
they say,
"It's not that simple."
They never realize
it has to be for me.

All that I have to pour,
to dash upon the greedy fire
is in that pail.

*There is a raging*

*i*

*There is a raging,*
*incoherent roar*
*of peoples' yearning.*
*All the voices cry*
*"Our blindness,*
*teach our blindness*
*how to see.*
*Our ears are stones,*
*our understanding dust.*
*Gives us the sounds.*
*Give us to understand."*

*They cease to speak*
*and in the unvoiced word*
*is harshness, stiffer than*
*the widest scream,*
*that pleads for them*
*a teaching tenderness*
*more necessary than*
*the taste of bread.*

*Their smooth eyes*
*turning to me*
*are a wall and there*
*against their rock,*
*their cutting edge,*
*I fall and beg*
*to find a gentle deafness,*
*go soft blind, and*
*pay no toll because*
*none is required.*

"Who is it?"
mechanically,
only the lips move.
Hands cover ears.
The answer
finds no entering.
No answer
is desired.
A face
gives lean sufficiency.
More
is a cluttering.
A face
is easy
to forget.

iii

If suddenly the world
should find me great,
or infamous, or
otherwise of use,
the quick, who pass me
in their clamor's flight,
would soon be pleased
to say they know me well.

They have of me these
two bright eyes, unclosed,
that look with longing
as we meet and pass,
(with haste, as they
insist our passing be,
that they
may take no hurt,
may dare no love)
our sterile capsules
sealed against the breath
of any other living,
needing self.
They would be pleased
to swear they touched my hands,
when what they caught
was nothing but a shade,
soft-tingeing, glancing,
ill-reflected hue,
upon their purposed shining's
barren rim where speed
and hardness answer
for all needs.

*iv*

*I may*
*turn to you*
*once again,*
*but with*
*another, newer,*
*older face*
*that knows*
*what you*
*must say,*
*what I*
*must hear,*
*what you*
*are not*
*and what*
*my heart*
*must bear.*

*Silent disclosure*

*There are
clear mysteries
so deep
I may not
speak of them
direct,
but I have
talked along
their edge
and done
no harm,
have turned away
and, silenced,
found a
consolation
less than kind.*

*The obvious for women*

*Surely our anatomy,*
*if not our wits,*
*should tell us that our role*
*is receptivity.*
*We are so clearly made*
*to welcome in*
*the physical, clean touch of love*
*and its dear seed,*
*and so inclined*
*by shape and aptitude*
*to harbor, nurture and enhance*
*the gift.*
*How sad for those*
*who choose to miss*
*the sense and symbol of a truth*
*that could not be more plain.*
*No woman's form on earth*
*can force its ultimate expression*
*on a man.*

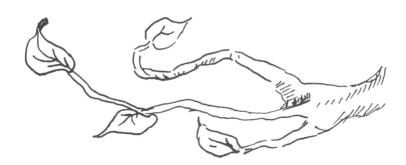

*The unfed*

*Life is uneven. It would seem*
*all dreamers die before the dream*
*is truth, and those who are unfit,*
*through lack of eagerness and wit,*
*have what was dearest to those dead*
*who had to leave with hearts unfed.*

*The tree—year 2034*

You can't imagine what I heard today.
One woman voted not to move the tree.
She voted not to cut it down.
She wants it left alone until it dies,
whenever that may be.

She lives just fifty miles
from a fresh air dispensary,
and there she is, talking about
how nature used to purify the air
when she was young.

She's quite old now. I know you've never heard of her.
I think you know the section where she lives,
in Megalopolis Nineteen,
close to the junction of the Interstates
Twenty-Six Thousand Nine and Seven Three Eight O.
The permanent earth covering's still lovely there.
It's of the early kind, soft-colored green
for restfulness and lack of glare.
A modern park was built some time ago,
just full of colored plastic forms and flashing lights.
Her room's in such a fine complex,
I can not see why she must think
of one old tree and want it left alone.
It's bound to die.

I saw a tape about the trees one time.
I guess you know, they never stayed the same.
Year after year at certain times the leaves came off,
and fell in piles like trash, and had to be swept up.
And then, at other times, warm times called spring,
there was a powder on the trees' new leaves.
To breathe the substance made some people ill.
And in between those times the trees were bare,
just great dark, straggly things above the ground,
not good for anything.
Imagine keeping something like that tree alive,
just to enjoy, as she proposed.

Of course, the vote went well,
the tree will be removed, a model made
of its statistics to be stored on tape.
Someone must show some sense about these things,
and most of us are very practical, I'm glad to say.

*There is a Day Star rising for men's hearts.*
*We may accept His brilliance as our own,*
*and yet, repeatedly we choose to keep*
*within the rayless night (our way made known*
*by random sparks struck from dark stone)*
*thinking we know exactly who we are,*
*insisting that we like to be alone*
*and fearing all the while to fall asleep.*

*Reality*

*We, man, the astronauts*
*ascended stepless air,*
*seeking the quiet moon*
*whose face we had adored*
*milleniums before.*
*We had, in all our lives,*
*yearned toward that face*
*as beauty magnified.*
*In aching flight*
*our eyes found moon to be,*
*as dry, as dry, as dry*
*and, turning back, saw earth*
*more beautiful*
*than that which we desired,*
*more beckoning*
*than all unmisted moons*
*and smaller*
*than we cared to understand.*

*The awakening*

*The only life of any bird is song.*
  *So from the brittle-boned, soft-feathered,*
   *open-beaked beginning*
    *all the necessary bugs with tissue wings*
   *are brought to strengthen him toward song*
    *which must fly, float and fall*
     *because he lives.*

*In this dark night*
  *when every song I could devise*
   *has been lived silently*
    *all through the day*
     *to those who hear and to the deaf,*
  *and I am still*
   *to gather strength*
    *for other songs*
     *I do not know,*

*I come awake*
  *and hear*
 *a dozen perfect melodies*
   *spring from the heart*
    *of one high-perching, heedless bird.*

All that he knows is sung
      with joy into the earless night,
   and he will sing again
         tomorrow after dark
       whether or not
            I hear.

A waiting poem
struggles in my mind,
moves like a dream
that seeks a dreamer
and finds all men awake.

How many poems,
unembodied, mute, are there
in mankind's noisy history,
unwritten
for the lack of solitude?

*Twice-fallen snow*

The barren trees no blossom touched in spring
bore flowerets dropped from the silent sky.
Snow lined each branch with icy blossoming
before the morning's winter sun was high.

Day warmed the branches with a silver light
until each crystal petal fell away,
and sight of falling snow, denied by night,
was mine because I yearned for it by day.

*The message*

*Hebrews 1:2 . . . in the last of the days He has*
*spoken to us in Son . . . Amplified Bible*

    *He spoke to us in Son,*
    *in mankind-language,*
    *in Christ Jesus,*
    *all of God that we could understand,*
    *and this is what I heard:*

    *"Child, you may choose*
    *to love me if you will,*
    *or you may see me,*
    *God-man, crucified for you,*
    *and look away."*

    *Such choice,*
    *such possibility*
    *is love defined.*

    *Not that He gave Himself*
    *into the limits of the human life,*
    *not that He willed to die for mankind's sake,*
    *but that He gives us opportunity*
    *to look upon the universes' only God*
    *and choose not to respond.*